dare to lead

THE CHALLENGE OF
BEING OUT IN FRONT

lucie harding

CONISTON DESIGNS

Today much is said about encouraging leadership, but anyone aspiring to it will often find the way blocked by those already in supposed leadership positions.

In modern business, many techniques are employed to ensure no one is in a position to challenge a leader. This self-serving nonsense is used by the weak and insecure.

A true leader is always ready to support and encourage someone who shows leadership potential.

Real leaders know their limitations and their shortcomings. They are willing to acknowledge their imperfections, if only to themselves.

Genuine leaders know they stand alone, and have the strength of mind to accept it. Leaders might have supporters, but in the end a leader must be the one out front.

Confidence in self is fundamental to the success of a leader. An understanding of your strengths is vital to achieving your goal.

Trust in others is important to a leader. If you cannot trust your associates, your friends, or others, success will always elude you.

Your confidence in others might not always be well founded, but mistakes are inevitable when dealing with human nature.

Do not be afraid of making a mistake.
Failures, as well as successes, are
building blocks on which leadership
quality stands.

When you attain leadership you are entitled to the benefits that go with it, as well as the responsibilities.

Benefits are personal to you alone.
Those you lead should not be placed
in a position of avarice or envy for
the things you have achieved.

With leadership comes great responsibility. You cannot escape this, nor can you unload it on to your subordinates.

As a leader you are responsible to those who reward you, whatever form your leadership takes. The reward might be monetary; or it might be more ephemeral, such as praise or fame.

Your greatest responsibility is for the welfare of those you lead. They might not have the qualities you possess, and thus you are honour bound to show them fairness, firmness and honesty.

You are also responsible to those who rely on you and your subordinates for support and direction. It is likely that these are the people whose goodwill ensures you remain a leader.

Lead by example and fairness. Those who lead by fear will enjoy only fleeting success. Oppressed and fearful people will rebel, sooner rather than later.

Tread a fine line between being a friend and being a leader. In the end you will stand alone, and authority will work far better than friendship.

However, a true leader needs friends. Ensure you maintain firm and loyal friendships unconnected with your leadership role.

Never be afraid of asking questions —
it is not a show of weakness. Even the
best leader cannot know everything.
Leadership is a process of continuing
self-education.

Seek the advice of those you lead. Each of them has special talents and abilities on which you depend. True leaders rely on those they lead to deliver a cohesive team.

A leader should not show preference to any one member of the team. Always encourage a person to develop special talents, but do it in a way that does not invite criticism from the less talented.

Be consistent in your leadership. It is important that those you lead understand what you require of them. Constant changes or variations along the way will only destroy teamwork, and you will lose their respect.

Be fair, be honest, be consistent, be
flexible, keep learning, take an interest
in the world around you and in the
people you lead, and you will be
rewarded by being considered a
true leader of people.

Dare to Lead
A Coniston Gift Book

Published by Coniston Designs
An Electra Media Group Enterprise

483 Green Lanes, London N13 4BS
Suite 204, 74 Pitt Street, Sydney NSW 2000
1133 Broadway, Suite 706, New York NY 10010

www.conistondesigns.com
giftbooks@conistondesigns.com

ISBN 0 86435 066 X

Printed in China

Images
Brand X Picture Arts